Lucy Cummings Smith

Lines

Lucy Cummings Smith

Lines

ISBN/EAN: 9783337312701

Printed in Europe, USA, Canada, Australia, Japan

Cover: Foto ©Thomas Meinert / pixelio.de

More available books at **www.hansebooks.com**

BY

L. C. S.

BISHOP   PRINCE'S PLACE, BRIGHTON.

———

1883.

To those who knew the beloved writer of the following Poems, no word need be said, for this little volume will receive at their hands an eager welcome; and, to all who had not that privilege, it is yet earnestly hoped that it may bring a " word in season :" for she " being dead, yet speaketh."

C. W.

Brighton.

August. 1883.

"Love is of God."

NOT ALONE!

COMPANIONS fair had I, while, as a child,
    I danced along the smooth ascent to youth,—
Light-footed Joy, brave Hope, and Fancy wild,
    With wondrous fairy tales, all told for truth.
Love too was near, and came at every call,
Flung kisses and fond words to great and small :
But of Love's nature then I scarce took note at all.

Companions these, along youth's level way,
    Hope, now the dearest, never left my side—
But Joy and Fancy would not always stay,
    And Love, drawn closer, proved with pain allied :
No longer gave she freely as of yore,
But set a price upon her priceless store,
And, e'en when best repaid, in secret pined for more.

B

2

Companions still are these, although I find

   The path grow narrow as my steps descend;

Joy, Hope, and Fancy sometimes lag behind—

   Let them ! so Love keep by me to the end !

Love changed and chasten'd—careless grown of sway,

Careless how any prize her or repay;

Caring for this alone—*to give herself away !*

From " Good Words." Sept., **1870**

3

UNDER THE PALMS.

I.

LED on—not driven by mere outward force ;
  Led on—not drifting at my own weak will ;
For falt'ring footsteps, an appointed course,
  For nerveless grasp, a Hand firm holding still.

Led on—past childhood's easy, grassy ways,
  Past youth's glad scaling of a flower-fringed steep,
Past plans and failures of less sanguine days,
  Past graves, where I had thought to stay and weep.

Led on ; but how ? I stumble as I go.
  Led on ; but whither ? clouds seem all I see.
My trust, a purpose higher than I know,
  My hope, a goal yet undescried by me.

Oh, friends ! if loved ones love me to the last,

And deem earth sadder for that I am gone,

Think not too much of the dim track I've passed,

Think still of me as but led on—*led on !*

January 31st, 1869.   Brighton.

II.

IN the band of noble workers
   Seems no place for such as I ;
They have faith where I have yearning,
   They can teach where I but sigh ;
They can point the road distinctly,
   Where for me the shadows lie.

Lofty purpose, high endeavour,
   These are not ordained for me :
Wayside flower may strive its utmost,
   It can ne'er become a tree,—
Yet a child may laugh to gather,
   And a sick man smile to see.

And I, too, in God's creation,

Have my little proper part ;

He must mean some service surely

For weak hand and timid heart,

Transient joys for my diffusing,

For my healing, transient smart.

Just to fling a ray of comfort

O'er life's downcast, dreary ways!

Just to fan a better impulse

By a full and ready praise ;

Pitying where I may not succour,

Loving where I cannot raise !

February 4th, 1869. Brighton.

III.

WHY would you have me dwell on death,

    Rehearse the awful parting hour,

    The creeping chill, the ebbing power,

The gasping for the latest breath?

Why vex a child 'neath noon-tide sky

    With image of his nightly rest?

    Just now his games, his toys, seem best--

He will be weary by and bye!

Just now a hand is linked in mine;

    Just now thought flashes far and free;

    I joy in everything I see;

I call *this* God-made world Divine!

Wait—till night fall at His behest,

    Wait—till He hush to sleep through pain,

    Wait—till He show me Death is gain,

And give the longing, with the power to rest.

February 4th, 1869.

8

IV.

NOT my will, gracious Lord,

 Not my blind will and wayward be fulfilled !

I dare not say that, bowing to Thy word,

All my heart's wishes are subdued and stilled.

My will might crave some boon by Thee denied,

Covet the praise that ministers to pride,

Shrink back from taking up a needed cross,

And shun the furnace to retain the dross.

Not my will, O my Lord.

No—be Thy name adored !

Though too much to the dust affection clings,

And self-wrought chains hold down the spirit's wings ;

Yet, out of sorrows past and present fears,

Out of experience bought by loss and tears,

At least the breathing of one prayer I've won,

Not my will, Father, but Thy will be done.

Dolhyfryd.
From " Good Words." 1869.

A GIRL'S FAITH.

NO two leaves above us waving
    Are quite like in form and hue,
No two flowers in equal measure
    Hold the blessing of the dew,—
Nothing is on earth repeated,
    All is special, all is new.

So of all the hosts of lovers,
    Now and in the days of yore,
Loving deeply, loving lightly,
    Loving less, or loving more,
None have loved—I hold it certain—
    Quite as you and I before !

Hearts have beat, but not as ours' did
  When this hope upon us broke :
All our former life mere dreaming,
  Till to consciousness we woke
In a world anew created,
  By a little word each spoke.

Not as ours! for that was needed,
  What belongs to us alone ;
Just the years we two have counted,
  Just the sorrows we have known,
Just your strength, and just my weakness—
  Love ! our love is all our own !

    Written for C——, June, 1869.
      From " Good Words." December, 1869.

A WIFE'S WONDER.

IF I had never met thee, my beloved,
    As in this world, where so much waste is seen,
    Or seeming waste, might easily have been,
I wonder what my nature would have proved !

I am so much thy work ; thy thoughts rule mine,
    Give them direction, lift from what is low ;
    What grasp or play of mind I have, I owe
To the strong happiness of being thine.

I catch thy tastes, enjoy what pleases thee,
    Learn what is beautiful from thy delight,
    Wait on thy choosing to decide aright ;
'Tis but thy shadow any praise in me.

To love, to pity, to forgive with ease,

    In others' hopes and fears to claim a part—

    Are but the o'erflow of a blissful heart,

And having *thee*, how should I fail in these?

If thou shouldst leave me!—in that utter woe

    I wonder what of life could still be mine!

    Would mind be quench'd, and heart grow cold with

        thine?

O God! forbid that ever I should know!

Bude.

From " Good Words." December, 1869.

THE WEDDING RING.

I CLIMBED the hill, and looked around—
The prospect stretched out wide ;
Green vales, rich woods, and shining sea—
Beauty on every side !

So fair, so far, so boundless all !
My spirit was oppressed ;
My glance roamed round, now here, now there,
And knew not where to rest.

Then from my finger, half in play,
My wedding ring I drew ;
And through that golden circlet small
Looked out upon the view.

I saw a wreath of cottage smoke,
　　A church spire rising by,
A river wind thro' sheltering trees,
　　Above—a reach of sky.

This little picture I had made
　　Both cheered and calm'd my soul;
True, I saw less, but what I saw
　　Was dearer than the whole.

More vivid lights, more solemn shades,
　　Such limits seemed to bring;—
My portion of the world be still
　　Framed by my wedding ring!

January, 1867. Suggested by lines of Grün.

IT does not show much in the hair, I allow,

   Nor does it perhaps very much in the brow ;

But it shows, ah ! of course, it must show in the skin,

Tho' it shows not at all in the feelings within ;

And it shows in the teeth which are no longer white,

And it shows in the eyes which are losing their light :

It shows in the waist which is no longer small,

It shows in the shoulders e'en seen thro' a shawl !

It shows in the lines round the lips that begin—

And it shows—oh ! ye pow'rs, *how* it shows in the chin !

What shows ? Never mind : there's no need to explain ;

All see it —*he* sees it, will see it again :

But he never has *said* it, that true heart of gold :

And so long as his arms his beloved one enfold,

So happy a creature can never be old !

WHAT *WAS.*

ONLY a burst of sunlight,
 To shine through a budding tree,
Only leaf-stars on the noon-tide blue,
 Yet a thrill of ecstasy !
And this is the spell works such wonders, beloved—
 'Tis the eyes of *two* that see.

Only the fire-light flicker
 On our plain green walls at play ;
And we, well shut in by storm without,
 At close of our third wet day.
" Can comfort, can cheeriness, go beyond this ? "
 So *two* happy voices say.

Only the same sweet life—

    Nothing startling, strange, and new ;

But we find fresh meaning and delight

    In the smallest thing we do ;

And the secret of this we have long agreed

    Is that everything's done by *two*.

WHAT *IS*.

ONE lonely creature dragging thro' her life,
　　Weeks long as months, and months stretched out
　　　　to years,
Waging with sorrow an unending strife,
　　Counting for sweetest solace, unchecked tears ;
All impulse, energy, and motive gone,
Nothing on earth to call or feel her own,
Nothing worth doing, since 'tis done alone.

This is the lot of one of that glad two !
　　The other's lot — but hope grows voiceless here,
Though ever straining for some nearer view
　　Of *his* high being in that "further sphere ;"
And pressing to her heart, thro' sharpest pain,
The thought that *he* for all his present gain,
Waits for the hour will make them *two* again.

M Y sorrow is my throne !

    It lifts me from the dust of earthly care ;

'Tis calm and peaceful, though so cold and lone—

    And wider prospects stretch before me there.

My sorrow is my crown !

    A glory round the worn and aching brow ;

I would not lay its thorny circlet down

    For any flowers earth has to offer now.

Yet sometimes I could deem

    I heard *his* voice, loved voice that guides me, say,

"The earth we loved must never trivial seem,

    Although our joy has passed from earth away."

" Go down, at my behest,

    The smallest, humblest, kindly task to do ;

I see the thorn-prints : hide them from the rest ;

    Because thou lov'st me *so*, ---love others too."

                           Edinburgh. 1875.

ALL MY DESIRE!

ALL I would wish from my loved one to hide,
    Take Thou away, Lord, take Thou away;
Meanness of jealousy, madness of pride,
    Take Thou away!

All I would be in that cherished one's sight,
    Make me to be, Lord, make me to be;
Faithful and loving, and true to the light,
    Make me to be!

Just as he lived, free from blame before all,
    Grant me to live, Lord, grant me to live;
Loyal to duty, whatever befall,
    Grant me to live!

Just as he died, on the heart he held dear,
    Give me to die, Lord, give me to die;
Meek, patient, calm—without shadow of fear,
    Give me to die!

SWEET, you were very far above me here,
    And yet you loved me in those by-gone days !
Not only fostering by your smile's bright praise
Such germs of good as might in me appear ;
But, with large insight, also holding dear
    My native, untaught, and impetuous ways.
    Now you are higher still; oh ! would you raise
Me if you might, to share your " further sphere ? "
My only loved ! I sometimes dare to think
    Such boundless joy would make me worthy thee,
That from thy side I should not fail or sink,
    Knowing thee happier thro' sustaining me.
Grow, blessed thought, grow strong ! then on the brink
    Of death, at least, I shall be anguish free.

As men born blind must ponder upon light,
   Deaf men on sound, though pondering seems vain ;
Since only *seeing* tells the joy of sight,
   And *hearing* only music can explain ;
   So I, beloved, must needs my spirit strain—
Long as endures life's dark and silent night—
   Some image of a future bliss to gain.

Knowledge will widen,—that must mean, for thee,
   God clearer seen in all His power has wrought ;
And oh ! my thinker, still more bold and free
   The range and energy of ceaseless thought.
High hopes are these ; but yet, for one like me,
   A simple image, with past rapture fraught,
Seems best to shadow forth what heaven may be.

Our life had days and years most glad and fair,

   Yet one joy thrills me still all joys above,

Because it rose on an almost despair—

   We two were parted ; should we meet ?   Oh ! Love,

I did not dare expect you,— *You were there !*

   That says it all ; and dying may but prove

A like surprise, and give me strength to bear.

        Dunkeld.   September 20th, 1875.

" Immortality is a great hope, but a dim conception."

W. S.

FROM the still sphere where dwells my highest hope,

    Stand off, I pray you, nor disturb the air !

Lest, while you boast it living, it should die,

    And I lose all, whose all is centred there.

Bring me no arguments, no reasoned proof;

    How if their weakness cloud that sacred trust ?

Leave it to God alone to mark its growth

    And keep it deathless—till I turn to dust.

Nor is this all—though more I dare not say,—

    Words would but marshal thoughts to endless strife;

Enough, if, cherished in my being's core,

    The silent hope may mould the lowly life.

Patterdale. December 19th, 1879.

WONDROUS head of some unknown departed,
  Caught by Art three hundred years ago—
Man so sad and yet so tender-hearted—
  This, at least, of thee we surely know,

That the strain of unremitting thinking
  Furrowed on thy brow those lines of pain ;
That a love from no self-torture shrinking
  Smiled a sweet acceptance of that strain.

Like, all tell me, to my one, my only,—
  Brother-souled I willingly agree,—
But my worship made that one less lonely,
  Nameless thinker, than thou seem'st to me.

Both have passed—one woman's heart left riven,—
  Both brave seekers now have gone up higher—
Found the truth—their spirits' only heav'n,
  Found in God—their infinite desire.

THE WAITING ROOM.

HOW well within the reach of all
    Life's precious things indeed !
The kindly word, the offering small,
    The slight, spontaneous deed.
What " New Year gift " could leave behind
    A sweeter trace than this—
A sudden impulse, good and kind,
    A country-woman's kiss?

The words exchanged were very few,
    Mere simple talk, no more ;
But each one's heart the other knew,
    A common garb we wore.
Her train came first, she took my hand,
    Held fast, and, saying this—
" We'll meet no more on earth," she gave
    A widow-woman's kiss !

" Diversely in many ways."

LIGHT the candles one by one,
    God's great work is but begun ;
Some were lighted long ago,
Caught at once the sacred glow ;
Others still unlighted stand,
Out of reach of mortal hand ;
Faculties undreamt of still,
Vaster knowledge, purer will.
These our faith may surely deem
Meant to catch the heavenly beam ;
When these kindle on their height,
Wide indeed the spread of light !
In the glory then displayed
Lights now prized may seem to fade ;

Let not this our hearts dismay,

One the source and *one* the ray.

" Diverse," but in place and name,

One the purpose of each flame ;

Light the candles, one by one,

God shall end what God begun.

St. Mary's, Edinburgh.

Christmas Day, 1880.

" DIVERSITIES OF GIFTS."

A S I wandered on the hill-side,
  Where the wild flowers spread and blow,
How I loved their simple faces,
  For the grace that each could show ;
Never asking for a likeness,
  As they were—I praised them so--
Some for beauty, some for fragrance,
  Some for whiteness, some for glow.

Oh, ye human flow'rs around me,
  I for you would feel the same !
Note each special gift for praising,
  Not each lack of gift for blame ;

Praise and own the pomp of colour,
  Scentless tho' the blossom flame,—
Own and love the lowliest leaflets
  That the gift of fragrance claim.

And the stunted growths among you,
  Scanty blossom, stem awry ;
Whether soil or season's doing,
  Tenderly I'll pass them by.
One sure proof they give of kin-ship—
  Like the best, they fade and die !
Who can tell ? some other summer
  With their beauty these may vie.

Patterdale.

"Seekest thou Great Things? Seek them not."

LITTLE rill of the mountain side, cushioned with
    moss,
Little rill that a baby's step safely might cross;
If I sit down beside you and listen for long,
I can just catch a gurgle, a tinkle, a song,
Grow distinct tho' so fairy faint—almost 'twould seem
Like an echo of music once heard in a dream.

Little rill, not far from you a stronger stream falls
Sheer down to the valley through steep rocky walls;
With a rapture of sound and a splendour of foam,
It bids its farewell to its lone early home;
And you, if you only could reach it, might blend
With its triumph, its daring, its course, and its end.

But I think, little rill, you will scarce get so far,

For the mosses half choke you up here where you are ;

And beyond I can see that the rushes grow high,

With their roots in a marsh and their stems stiff and

    dry.

They will need and exhaust you, you poor little rill,

You will end there unnoticed, your song will be still.

Never mind, little rill, moss and rushes will grow

All the greener and stronger because of your flow ;

And your cool, quiet current, tho' mostly unheard,

May yield draughts of fresh strength to some wing-

    weary bird ;

And, whene'er for a brief space unshadowed you run,

You can catch and give back the warm glints of the

    sun.

And the strong stream you hear—*tho' it cannot hear*

    you—

Is born just as you are—from rainfall and dew ;

And, for all its importance, its foam and its roar,

You are closely akin—'tis not *other*, but *more.*

Nay — is there indeed any great, any small,

In the sight of the INFINITE SOURCE of us all?

From " Day of Rest." *July*, 1879.

" Deep streams run still,--and why ? Not because there are
no obstructions, but because they altogether overflow
those stones or rocks round which the shallow stream
has to make its noisy way ; 'tis the full life that saves
us from the little noisy troubles of life."—W. S.

ECHOES.

DEEP the stream and silent—
Scarce I hear its flow—
What a noise its current
Made few days ago !

Round the stones it fretted
On its shallow way—
Babbling in vexation
Over each delay.

Came the heavy rainfall,
　　Swelled the river's might—
Now its stony troubles
　　Are unheeded quite.

So, when our complaining
　　Tells of constant strife
With some moveless hindrance
　　In our path of life ;

What we need is only
　　Fullness of our own—
If the current deepen,
　　Never mind the stone !

Let the fuller nature
　　Flow its mass above,
Cover it with pity,
　　Cover it with love.

" To love is the great glory, the last culture, the highest
happiness ; to *be* loved is little in comparison."

"*Gravenhurst.*"   *William Smith.*

THE MORE EXCELLENT WAY.

YES, the love that we get is a joy and a power—
'Tis as rain to the deep-thirsting root ;
As the sun-light to open and colour the flower ;
As the sun-warmth to ripen the fruit.
We will hail it and prize it so long as we live ;
But the life of the soul is the love that we give.

If the root underground be worm-stricken and dry,
If the flower have all withered away—

What avails that the soft rain still falls from the sky

   Or bright sun-beams be still at their play?

But from darkness and drought we may suffer, yet live ;

For the life of the soul is the love that we give.

From the " Day of Rest."

MOODS.

LORD, in Thy sky of blue,
  No stain of cloud appears ;
  Gone all my faithless fears,
Only Thy Love seems true.
Help me to thank Thee, then, I pray,
Walk in the light and cheerfully obey !

Lord, when I look on high,
  Clouds only meet my sight ;
  Fears deepen with the night ;
But yet it is Thy sky.
Help me to trust Thee, then, I pray,
Wait in the dark and tearfully obey.

Bude. 1869.

CLOUDS.

A CLOUD upon the sky !
  Flowers close their cups, the butterfly his wing,
  The restless birds cease all at once to sing,
The shiv'ring leaves foretell a shower is nigh.
  Let the grey evening darken into night !
  To-morrow's sun will only shine more bright,—
    Such clouds as this pass by !

A cloud upon the brow !
  A palsy of the thoughts so free before,
  A sense of effort never known of yore,
A sudden change 'twixt yesterday and now.
  If we would scan it, it eludes the sight,
  And yet our spirits own its subtle might.
    Will this cloud pass, and how ?

A cloud upon the heart !

What pleased so late has lost its charm to-day ;
The trust undoubting seems misplaced and bold,
The kindly words sound distant, stiff, and cold ;
The form remains, the life has pass'd away,
Each shrouded spirit acts its former part,
Smile still meets smile, but heart is far from heart.
Will this cloud e'er depart ?

What brought the clouds we mourn ?

Was it some truth out-spoken, love should hide ?
Some want of reverence in a playful mood—
Some thought confided and not understood—
Some chill to feeling, or some shock to pride ?
Enough--they're risen—grief and tears are vain,
After the darkness and the bursts of rain,
Such clouds as these return !

A SUDDEN storm has swept our summer bowers,
    The grass is snow-flaked with the blossoms shed ;
We deem the wind that ravaged thus the flowers
    Must needs have struck the marring weed-growth
        dead.
Alas ! the fragrant and the fair are gone;
We mourn their loss—but still the weeds live on !

The storm of sorrow o'er our hearts has swept,
    Our life is wither'd, and our hopes are slain ;
We think the bitter tears that we have wept
    Must needs have wash'd away the spirit's stain,—
That selfish jealousy and haughty pride,
With better, brighter things, have surely died.

That henceforth what of chasten'd love we own

   Shall all divine in aim and nature be,

Without an earthly hope to drag it down,

   Mighty to soar on high, serene and free ;

No shadow cast by self to darken there—

A quiet sympathy — a constant pray'r.

Alas, the weeds the storm has spared ! the while

   It laid our fragrance and our beauty low ;

The day is dark, unlighted by a smile,

   The hours, unmark'd by word of fondness, slow.

The heart's insatiate still, though sad and lorn,—

The storm that marr'd the flower has left the thorn !

A FACT.

IT was on an English summer day,
　　Some six or seven years ago,
That a pointsman before his cabin paced
　　With a listless step and slow.
He lit his pipe—there was plenty of time—
　　In his work was nothing new :
Just to watch the signals and shift the points
　　When the next train came in view.

He leant 'gainst his cabin, and smoked away,—
　　He was used to lounge and wait ;
Twelve hours at a stretch he must mind those points,
　　And down trains were mostly late !

A rumble—a roar—" She is coming now—
　　She's truer to time to-day !"
He turns,—and, not far off, between the rails,
Sees his youngest boy at play !

Not far, *but too far*.　The train is at hand,
　　And the child is crawling there,
And patting the ground with crows of delight—
　　And not a moment to spare !
His face was dead white, but his purpose firm,
　　As straight to his post he trod,
And shifted the points, and saved the down train,
　　And trusted his child to God !

There's a rush in his ears, though the train has passed ;
　　He gropes, for he cannot see,
To the place where the laughing baby crawled,
　　Where the mangled limbs must be.

But he hears a cry that is only of fear—

His joy seems too great to bear,

For his duty done, God saw to his son—

The train had not touched a hair !

From " Good Words." May, 1871.

TO C———.

CHRISTMAS, 1878.

SWEET fervent soul—so warm, so bright,
　　So prompt with smile or tear ;
Worthy all love—but in *my* sight
　　Thro' *love of him* most dear.

No other thought, no other name,
　　My deepest feelings wake—
Nor would I urge another claim,
　　Than " Love me for his sake !"

TO M———.

CHRISTMAS, 1880.

MY almost child from far-off days,
　　One thing I wish you good and new,
" The giftie," in the poet's phrase,
　　" To see yoursel' as others see you."

For I have marked your spirits fall,
　　From taking quite a private view—
When you—who else are just to all,
　　W'ont " see yoursel' as others see you."

Oh sweet flower-face, believe our gaze—
　　Leal heart, quick wit, accept your due—
Truth still is true in garb of praise,
　　Just " see yoursel' as others see you."

CHRISTMAS CARD.

To U. and A.

DEAR birds, so close upon one bough,
    A tranquil sky above you—
Be ever more as close as now,
    So pray the hearts that love you.

The sky indeed may cloud or change,
    There is no trust in weather !
And you may seek a lowlier range,
    But you will fly together.

Together build and tend the nest,
    Together soar on high,
And, having known earth's very best,
    Dear birds, together die !

CHRISTMAS CARD FOR THE OLD.

(With picture of a Robin)

OUR other birds sing best in Spring,
  Their song is of delight,
Of nestlings safe beneath the wing,
  Of love, of joy, of light !

The robin sings when trees are bare
  And cold and dull the scene—
No mate, no nestlings, claim his care,
  He sings of what has been.

And we, who walk in dreary ways
  And find them lone and long,
May still look back to happier days
  And bless the Robin's song !

CHRISTMAS DAY.

LET us turn from private troubles,
Give our thoughts a wider scope ;
Look out to man's higher future —
Christmas tells of Hope !

If a jar, a discord, vex us,
We will bid its turmoil cease ;
Every voice to-day be tender !
Christmas tells of Peace !

If our cherished ones have left us,
Through our tears we'll look above ;
Love is deathless as its giver !
Christmas tells of Love !

NEW YEAR'S DAY.

WHAT will the New Year bring?
　　What take away?
　Seek not to guess its course,
　　Live in to-day.

Do to-day's duty,
　　Prize its delight,—
Then, when to-morrow comes,
　　All will be right.

Love those around you now,
　　Better and best :
"Live like Immortals here ; "
　Trust for the rest.

THOUGHTS FOR THE OLD YEAR.
TRUE RICHES.

A S we near the dark river, so deep and so strong,
  The river we all have to cross,
How our treasures drop off as we journey along,
  How much of our gold turns out dross !
All the sense of distinction, the subjects of pride,
  Seemed part of our being before,
Are so scared at the rush of that pitiless tide,
  They leave us alone on its shore.

But the love in our hearts and the memories pure
  Of all that was tender and true,
Through the last weary steps of our journey endure,
  Nor fade with the river in view.
We can carry them safely quite down to its brink,
  They suffer no change and no loss ;
And the river need hardly affright if we think,
  Perhaps—we shall take them across !

NEW YEAR WISHES.

GOOD NEW YEAR WISHES for my friends!
    Good New Year Wishes truly !
I feel my heart beat high with these,
    Yet cannot speak them duly.
The very phrases others use
    Half jar upon my ear ;
They seem to miss my inmost thought
    Of blended hope and fear.

" A happy year, with many more
    To follow in its train ! "
So runs the hackneyed form, as though
    Long life to all were gain !

As though bright suns had only power
  To colour, not to fade !
As though no growth of human flower
  Were fairest in the shade !

My many friends, I dare not breathe
  A common wish for all !
A honeyed thought to *you* or *you*
  To others were but gall.
So different the heart within,
  The outward life around,
You scarcely see the self-same sky,
  Or tread the self-same ground.

There are who wake from troubled sleep,
  This birthday of the year,
To feel their anguish but renewed
  By sounds of general cheer :—

Some voice is still that greeted them
 On last year's opening day—
Some eyes that dwelt on their's with love
 In Earth are put away.

Last year had days and nights that passed
 In sorrow soothed by sharing ;
Now there is none to soothe and bless
 By calm and cheerful bearing !
Their eyes may weep to dimness now—
 No further need for hiding !
Of smiling back their loving flow,
 For fear of loving chiding !

There are, to whom a cup of joy
 So foaming o'er is given,
It seems too full for Life to drain—
 It seems as Earth were Heaven !

They fain would fling their weight of bliss
   On Time's too rapid flying,--
Stretch the glad moments into years,
   And stay the years from dying !

There are whom still the Future lures
   From present pastures fair,
With promise of a fuller life,
   With whispered " Then !" and " There ! "
Their hope-lit " Now " seems cold and slow,
   They pray to Time, " Speed fleeter !
Set—summer suns ! pass—tranquil hours !
   And make our bliss completer ! "

And there are others, who foresee
   Throughout the coming year,
No rainbow in their leaden sky,
   No special hope or fear :—

Their morrows tell the tale inscribed
  On yesterday's dull page ;
No wayside flower to mark the path
  That leads from youth to age.

My many friends, how should I find
  A wish ye all might share?
I dare not utter one at all,—
  Or only as a Prayer—
That He who knows each spirit's wants
  Beyond my love to read,
May mould your wishes to His will,
  And crown them thus indeed :—

May give the lonely—patient hearts
  The weight of Life to bear ;
May nerve the loving and beloved
  The thought of Death to dare !—

Before you all One Presence go,

    To guard and guide you right ;

To some, the pillared cloud by day,

    To others, " Light by Night ! "

From " Good Words." 1861.

EXCELSIOR.

IF you yourself stand low, the low will hide from you
the high ;

Rise, and the topmost peaks alone are out-lined on
the sky.

Yet even so, you say, a cloud may hide them from
your sight ;

Still *Rise*—nor count it labour lost—that cloud pro-
claims their height.

Llanberis. 1876.